AN INTERPRETATION OF THE ARTWORKS IN ST. FRANCIS OF ASSISI CHURCH — FITCHBURG, MA

by

Angelo J. Bisol Sr. (1924 – 2001)

Edited:

JOHN L. BISOL

AN INTERPRETATION OF THE ARTWORKS in St. Francis of Assisi Church – Fitchburg, MA

1st Edition

Compiled and Edited for St Francis of Assisi Parish by:
Angelo Joseph Bisol Sr.   1999©

2nd Edition

FOREWORD

by

John L. Bisol

There has been a familial attachment to St. Francis of Assisi Paris of Fitchburg, MA and the Bisol family since my grandparents, John and Angela, settled nearby on Nichols Street in the early 1900's. Four of my Aunts were so comforted and inspired by the parish, the community, and the setting, that they chose to serve Our Lord as Sisters in the Venerini Order – and three of them continue to do so as of this writing!

I attended services for a large part of my life at St. Francis parish, as did my four brothers and six sisters. My father served Mass there, as a young boy, in this church he always knew as his. In later years he devoted much of his time to the "Mechanics" of running the parish; setting the altar, creating candleholders in his woodshop, opening the church doors, assisting at Masses…always busy, but never in the forefront.

He had an inspiration after my mother's death to document the beauty of the church building. He did this not to assume the building to be more important than the community itself, but to capture in some way the "instructional nature" of this majestic building and its art, lest such knowledge be lost. He died two years after finishing the first edition.

During his funeral Mass, I was asked to lead the "Prayers of the Faithful" and I dutifully went to the lectern at the appointed time. There were no written prayers on the usual shelf, but without missing a beat, I led the community in five prayers of my own choosing. Later that day, my aunt commented how it was that "Angelo (my father), always left the Prayers on the Lectern. He was so thorough about preparing for the Mass."

I simply answered that my father HAD left the prayers at the lectern that day – ME!

Finally, there are no "pictures" in this book. In order to thoroughly enjoy the artwork, you must view it firsthand, in the solemnity of the church, preferably on a sunny day – the better to appreciate the effects of light on the murals and windows.

DOMUS MEA DOMUS ORATIONIS VOCABITUR[1]

"My House Shall Be Called A House Of Prayer": Isiah 56: 7
Inscription over the main doors to the church.

(The following is paraphrased from the St. Francis of Assisi 75th anniversary book)

On September 17, 1903, the Feast of the Stigmata of Saint Francis of Assisi, the parish family was born and placed under the patronage of the saint whose glorious sufferings were remembered on that day.

The following Sunday, at all the Masses as parishioners of Immaculate Conception Parish, it was announced that the new parish would have Father Louis-Alfred Langlois as its first pastor in South Fitchburg.

Few today can recall those earliest days, but the parish spirit that is enjoyed to this day makes it easy to imagine how very happy was the first meeting of the new pastor with the first parishioners of St. Francis.

They met for the first time on Monday, September 21, 1903, in the family home of Mr. Alfred Barrette, with Mr. Paul Lafleur presiding. Warm words of welcome and tokens of appreciation were tended the new pastor as the community took its first steps in joy and hope.

It must be recognized that St. Francis would not be the community it is today had not this brief but hearty welcome been immediately

---

[1] Inscription above the Outside Main Entrance Doors to St. Francis of Assisi Parish

followed by a meeting in the hall of the "Club Moreau." Here, the pastor of Immaculate Conception Parish announced a gift of the land on Sheridan Street for the new parish. A committee of 20 was chosen to help develop the organization of the parish. The priority item on the agenda of that first parish meeting was the construction of a Chapel School. That first dream would soon be realized thanks to fund-raising bazaars and the like and the inspiring leadership of Father Langlois, who showed himself very sensitive to the needs of his new parish family from the very first day.

There were indeed many challenges that awaited the young parish and its new pastor. But it had clearly become necessary to establish a parish in South Fitchburg. At the turn of the century, there were some 200 families living in the area of the Falulah Paper Company, Culley Saws, Shirreff Woolen Mill, the Boston and Maine Railroad, and many smaller industries. In those days, transportation was a serious problem and many families found themselves unable to attend Mass on Sundays and Holy Days.

As early as 1902, Father J. E. Marcoux, the pastor of Immaculate Conception Parish, began to prepare a division of his parish to better serve the needs of his people in South Fitchburg. Fr. Marcoux had purchased and developed an 80,000 sq. ft. plot of land on Sheridan Street at the cost of $1500. As he was preparing a school for the children who lived a mile and a half from the city schools, Bishop Thomas D. Beaven of Springfield responded to a request from the people of South Fitchburg and assigned Father Langlois to found a new parish here.

By 1903, the many Franco-Americans then living in Fitchburg found their religious lives revolving around three parishes: Immaculate Conception, the oldest parish, founded in 1886; and two daughter parishes, Saint Joseph, founded in 1890, and the new St. Francis of Assisi. The distances separating the center of the city from the western section and the southern section and the fact that many families found themselves living in the industrial areas of these three sections had brought about these foundations.

One of Father Langlois' first tasks was the Parish Visitation, which was to become a regular event in the parish. In this first census, the concerned Father learned that he had in his care 1,068 souls who made up 200 families.

As the years passed and the humble foundation of 1903 blossomed into a flourishing parish, the original Chapel-School was no longer sufficient for the needs of the parish that had doubled in size.

The first glimmerings of the new church appeared in January of 1920. Then, a general drive that came to be called "la Grande Campagne" was announced to pay off the parish debt and to lay the foundations for the new church. It was Father Henri Lasagna, associate pastor at the time, who organized this important step, which was to unleash a chain of happy events in the parish.

By April of 1925, proposals for the new church and what it would mean to the parish were outlined to the parishioners. Once the church was built, the chapel would become entirely classrooms, providing a total of eight rooms in the school building, with two additional classrooms at the rectory. The proposed cost of the church, without decorations, ranged from $100,000 to $125,000. The parish could assume a debt of $75,000; if work went well, in three years they would amass another $50,000.

Built at an additional cost of $150,000, the stained glass windows and other glass works were supplied by Von Gerichten Art Glass Company, of Munich, Germany. The interior decorations, (artworks) were done by Professor Gunippo Raggi, Rome, Italy. The organ is by Casavant Freres, St. Hyacinte, Quebec, Canada.

This Interpretive Guide is offered with the expectation that it will answer many of the questions a visitor to St Francis of Assisi Parish might have. In addition, in some measure, the Interpretive Guide may help the visitor appreciate "the artworks that surround you".

Sacred Art and Sacred Furnishings

Before we discuss St. Francis of Assisi church as it is constructed in Fitchburg, MA, several architectural prominences must be understood in the general context of the Catholic celebration of the Mass.

The "Church" has not adopted any particular style of art as her own. She has admitted styles from every period, in keeping with the national characteristic and conditions of peoples and the needs of the various rites.

Because the assembly gathers in the presence of God to celebrate His saving deeds, liturgy's climate is one of awe, mystery, wonder, reverence, thanksgiving, and praise. Therefore, it cannot be satisfied with anything less than the "beautiful" in its environment and in all its artifacts, movements, and appeals to the senses.

The Sanctuary

(The most sacred part of a place in a sacred structure)
The Sanctuary should be distinguished from the rest of the church by some feature such as a raised floor, a special shape, or notable decoration. It should be large enough for the sacred rites to be performed without difficulty.

The Altar

The altar, on which the Sacrifice of the Cross is made present under Sacramental signs, is also considered the Lord's Table from which the people are invited to share when they come to celebrate the Mass as a community. The main altar should be free standing, away from any wall, so that the priest (celebrant) can walk all around it, and can celebrate facing the assembled people (congregation). It should be in a position such that the entire congregation will naturally focus their attention on it.

Adornments of the Altar

Out of reverence for the Mass, which is both a sacrifice and a sacred meal, the altar must be covered with at least one cloth – usually white. A second covering, colored and/or with design(s) on it matches the liturgical-year calendar or the event (Baptism, Confirmation, Marriage, Funeral).

In all liturgical celebrations, candles are required to express reverence, and to indicate the various degrees of solemnity. The candles must not impede the people's view of the altar or of anything placed on it.

A cross, easily visible to the people, should be on the altar or somewhere not far from it. This cross may be "portable" in that it can be used to lead procession/recession from the altar or for special services.

The Celebrant's Chair and other Seats

The Celebrant's Chair should draw attention to his office - of presiding over the gathered community and leading its prayer. The Chair of that person should be clearly in a presiding position, although it should not suggest domination or remoteness. There may be other seats, placed beside the celebrant's or pews for the liturgical participants, but none shall be primary to the Celebrant's Chair.

The Ambo

The Ambo, or lectern, is a standing desk for reading and preaching (although preaching may be done from the chair or elsewhere - one main Ambo should be reserved for these functions). Like the altar, it should be beautifully designed, constructed of fine materials, and positioned carefully and simply for its function. The Ambo represents the dignity and uniqueness of the Word of God and of reflection upon that Word.

St. Francis of Assisi – Fitchburg, MA

Upon entering St. Francis of Assisi Church for the first time, the visitor may feel somewhat unsettled, first for the volume of the structure alone and second the sense of solitude and tranquility portrayed by its massive build.

A first glance might suggest nothing out of the ordinary for a Catholic church, but upon closer examination, there is a marvelous story to tell. The contrasting colors of the stained glass windows, each affected by the light in a unique way. are very inspiring and devotional.

From the Nave, looking straight ahead beyond the magnificent baptismal font, one sees a simple altar with a majestic back ground of white marble and superbly crowned by a huge window depicting the Crucifixion of Christ.

The rising morning sun transforms this scene into a three-dimensional view so impressive that once seen, it is long remembered.

In the center of the window, the figure of Christ's body hangs from the cross in the slump of death. Around the cross, are the witnesses present at Calvary. Alone, to the left, stands the derider in the presence of the Centurion and the believers, including the Virgin Mother, Mary Magdalene, St. John, and others.

The earthquake and darkness mentioned in the Scriptural narrative by St. Luke is also in evidence, as is intense emotion and a sense of utter chaos.

A banner interwoven above the cross in Latin translates:

"BEHOLD THE LAMB OF GOD WHO TAKES A WAY THE SINS OF THE WORLD".

Other characters depicted in this window are the literal symbols of the four evangelists: to the left, a <u>Young Man,</u> (Matthew) and <u>Lion,</u> (Mark); to the right an <u>Ox,</u> St. Luke and an <u>Eagle,</u> St. John. At the center top left, the inscription *I.H.S.*, a monogram of the name Jesus derived from the Greek. At the center, top right, a Chalice and Host, symbolic of the body and blood of Christ.

On the extreme left side, a small panel depicts the face of Christ on Veronica's veil; and a window on the left side in a small panel above the cross, a crown of thorns. On the extreme right side, there is a small panel, showing the tools of the Crucifixion - Hammer, nail and tongs, also scourging pillar and whips.

From the Nave and facing the altar, to the left, and right of the grand window of "the Crucifixion", are two almost rectangular painted panels depicting the four so-called <u>Latin</u> doctors of the Church. Canonized Saints who have made <u>notable contributions</u> to the Church by their <u>writings</u> and <u>teachings</u> may be declared "Doctors of the Church". Much of their writings and teachings were against the heresy of their day. Heresy remains one of the most serious sins, because it destroys faith, the very foundation of eternal Salvation. The Heresies are listed below as a reference.

Arianism: was the principal heresy, which denied the divinity of Christ.

Monarchianism: taught that God is the Father, or the Son, or the Holy Ghost, according to what He is doing at the time.

Donatism: taught that baptism and other sacraments administered by an unworthy minister were invalid.

10

Monophysitism: taught that Christ had one single nature, not two distinct natures, one human and one divine.

Iconoclasm: (image-breaking) was the heretical movement, which taught that the veneration of images, pictures, and relics was idolatrous.

Montantism: imposed a rigorous moral code and proclaimed the immediate end of the world and the Second Coming of Christ.

Gnosticism: held that special knowledge, secretly revealed, was necessary for salvation.

Nestorianism: held that there were two persons, one human, and the other divine, in Christ.

Manichaeism: ascribed a twofold origin to life holding that matter is evil and that spirit is good, and that these two supreme principles are in constant conflict.

Pelagianism: denied the doctrine of original sin, the necessity of baptism and of grace for salvation.

In the Western (Latin) Church, four great doctors have been recognized. They were officially granted the title by decrees of Pope Boniface VIII in 1298 A.D.:

 St. Ambrose (397 A.D.), St. Augustine (430 A.D.) Jerome (420 A.D.) and Gregory the Great (604 A.D.). (The dates given are the dates of their deaths).

In the Eastern (Greek) church a similar development took place. In 1568 A.D., Pope Pius V honored four Eastern fathers with the same title:

Basil (379 A.D.); Gregory Naianzen (389 A.D.); John Chrysotom (407 A.D.) and St. Anthanasius (373 A.D.).

To the left, the panel depicts St. Jerome (the lion is pointing to him) and Pope St. Gregory the Great. To the right, the panel depicts the two other doctors of the Church, St. Ambrose, standing on the left and St. Augustine, on the right.

ST. JEROME

St. Jerome, priest and a Doctor of the church, was born about 342
A.D. in Stridon, a small town near Aguileia, Italy. He died in
Bethlehem, Palestine on September 30, 420 A.D.

Jerome's father Eusebius, a prosperous Christian landowner, enrolled
him at an early age in the local Christian Catachumenate to prepare
Jerome for Baptism.

Sent to Rome circa 360 A.D. for an education in the Classics, he
studied Latin and then Greek, devoting himself to oratory and finally
pleaded at the Bar. Among his teachers was one called Didymus, the
blind, who was the most distinguished figure from the greatest school
of theological opinion in the early church, "The Alexandrine School".
St. Jerome always treasured his classical training, forgetting all else.
For a time, he gave himself up to the world. But his piety returned to
him after he began to travel.

He traveled East and visited the Anchorites and other persons of
Sanctity.

He took up his abode in the desert of Chalcis in Syria where he spent
four years of prayer and study.

While fasting in the desert, Jerome had a dream in which Christ
appeared to him. Our Lord gently chided him for his great fondness
for classical authors; admonishing him, "Thou art a Ciceronian not a
Christian. Where thy heart is, there also is thy treasure."

Jerome departed for Rome, where he filled for some time, the office
of secretary to Pope St. Damasus. After the death of the Pope, Jerome

retired to Bethlehem. His solitary life at Bethlehem began a career of study, which has immortalized him.

His scriptural works, above all, have been unparalleled in the history of the church:

"…So great is the dignity of the soul, that each of them has an angel assigned for its protection from the moment it is born," he said. (Speaking on the spirituality of the faithful.)

"…If there is anything in this life which sustains a wise man and induces him to maintain his serenity amidst the tribulations and adversities of the world it is in the first place, I consider the meditation and knowledge of the Scriptures…"

ST. GREGORY THE FIRST

St. Gregory was born about 590 A.D. in Rome. The last of the great
Latin fathers of the Church, he cared for the poor of Rome and
protected them from invaders. He sent missionaries to England and
across Europe and made lasting contributions to the literature and
liturgy of the church.

He was the first Pope to make clear to the world that he headed the
entire Church. Gregory I was the outstanding pontiff of the early
medieval era. His extremely wealthy father, Gardianus, owned large
estates in Sicily in addition to a beautiful manor on the Coelian Hill in
Rome. During his boyhood, the Goths had despoiled Rome and the
population had dwindled; the life of the city had become
disorganized.

In spite of these adverse conditions, Gregory received an excellent
education and was noted for his proficiency in grammar, rhetoric, and
dialectic.

Because of his position among the aristocratic families, Gregory
entered public life and held a number of small offices. At the age of
33, he became prefect of the city of Rome, the highest civil office in
Roman political circles. Two year later, he resigned and
renounced his wealth to live a monastic life in his home.

He founded and endowed six other monasteries on his Sicilian estate.
About 578 A.D., he was made one of the seven deacons of Rome. He
served as ambassador to the Imperial Court in Constantinople.
When Pelagius died in 590 A.D., the clergy and people elected
Gregory, Pope.

Gregory managed the temporal affairs of the church with administrative skills. On the estates bequeathed to the church, he placed many skilled overseers who administered the land, and collected the rents. Gregory judged all grievances of the tenants. He used the revenues from the estates for the care of the poor, showing unfailing kindness to the large numbers of refugees who flocked to Rome. He also assumed the former obligation of feeding the needy. Gregory presented five major themes during his tenure.

I. On Broadening the Concent of the Papacy

- He strictly supervised all aspects of Church activity.
- His letters to various Bishops indicated his interest in those distant dioceses.
- He insisted that Priest observe the regulations forbidding them to marry.
- The Pope consistently used his influence to settle difficulties
- in dioceses far from Rome.
- The Pope approved council and Synod actions.

II. On Church and State

- He looked upon both Church and State as founded by God.
    - Each was to cooperate with the other to form a united whole.
    - Each, however, would remain supreme in its own sphere.

III. On the Jews

Church policy towards the Jews was developed during the Pontificate of Pope Gregory I, called Gregory the Great (509 A.D. - 604 A.D.). Recognizing the historical role of the Jews, Prophets, Apostles and Christ himself, Gregory hoped for eventual reconciliation and the Jewish acceptance of Christ. Gregory decreed:

"…We forbid you to molest the Jews or to lay upon them restrictions not imposed by established laws…"

IV. **On Liturgy and Literature** (The Gregorian Chant)

The liturgical chant that bears his name took definite form after some centuries of development. When the church was freed from persecution early in the fourth century, the need for formal public worship was soon apparent. Gregory I then issued a sacramentary, containing the celebrant's part of the Mass and an antiphony, with the choral parts for the Mass and other liturgical rites. Whether Gregory was himself a musician or merely approved the work of musicians is not known. Some historians credit him with compiling, codifying, and editing the chants.

V. **Breviary and Hymns**

The hymns for Sunday and the rest of the week are by one writer who according to tradition is St. Gregory the Great.

Matins: Morning Prayer

Lauds: Morning Hymns

Little Hours: Between Lauds and Vespers

Vespers: The evening counterpart of Lauds is Vespers

"*Alleluia!*" expresses joyful reactions to the word of God. It serves as either a response or introduction and symbolizes the endless joys of Paradise. (literally: Praise Yahweh)

Regina Coeli Laetare ("Joy to Thee O Queen of Heaven!") is an Easter song adapted from an older Christmas hymn. Its exact author is unknown and does not appear until the late 12th century.

According to "The Golden Legends", St. Gregory the Great heard the angels singing the Regina Coeli at the bridge of St. Angelo and adopted it for use. (It is a charming story, but unconfirmed). Antiphons of Our Lady are:

Alma Redemptoris Mater ("Mother Benign our Redeeming Lord").

Ave Regina Coelorum ("Hail O Queen of Heaven Enthroned").

Regina Coeli Laetare ("Joy to Thee O Queen of Heaven) and the Salve Regina, known universally in English as "Hail Holy Queen" which is a favorite among the four.

ST. AMBROSE

St. Ambrose was born in Trier, Germany in about 340 AD. Ambrose was called upon to play an active role in the civil and religious life of his day. He died in Milan, Italy where he had served as Bishop for 23 years on April 4, 397 AD.

His father was the prefect of Galli and Ambrose was given a thorough training in Greek, Latin and the law.

His early legal success brought him to the attention of Emperor Valentinian, who appointed him governor of Liguria and Aemilia with a residence at Milan.

Christians and Arians struggled for control of the area. In 374 AD., when the seat became vacant, the Emperor was called upon to fill the seat. Valentinian refused, ordering the elections to proceed in the customary way; that is, by the vote of the assembled clergy and laity. When the Christians met in the basilica, Ambrose was chosen by popular acclamation.

At this time, Ambrose was still a Catechumen. One week after his baptism, Ambrose was consecrated as a Bishop. During the following decade, Ambrose became the indefatigable defender of the true faith. The struggle between the Bishop and the Arian government reached its climax in 385 AD., when Ambrose prevented the imperial family from entering the basilica for Arian worship.

Milan's Bishop had the support of the populace at-large. Throughout the crisis, St. Ambrose was essentially a practical man. In spite of the demands of political necessity, Ambrose found time to write extensively and ably of the Christian truths, <u>as a practical Shepherd.</u> <u>not as a speculative Theologian.</u> Homilies, (sermons on Scripture), were copied down by listeners and later published.

The custom of using hymns, which was also known as "Private Psalms", was introduced into the West in the fourth century. St. Hilary (315 AD. - 367 AD.) and Ambrose were the two earliest composers.

The hymns of St. Ambrose were profound in thought and infused with spirituality nevertheless, simple in construction and wording; they became very popular. Many other unknown poets imitated the model set by St. Ambrose and these hymns are therefore known as *Ambrosiani*.

The *Exultet* is a development of the prayer of the blessing of the lights, which formed part of the ancient *Lucernarium* (a lighting of candles or lamps). The early church did not bless things the way they are blessed today: They blessed God who gave the gift of the light, and then they gave the light back to him.

Gradually one single text was adopted throughout the church, this is the present *Exultet*, which has been attributed both to St. Augustine (354 A.D. - 430 A.D.) and to St. Ambrose (340-397 A.D.), - and therefore its true author is not definitely known.

Concerning the tradition of the Immaculate Conception, St. Ambrose - writing in the fourth century - gave witness that belief in Mary's freedom from sin was current in the early church.

"...Receive me, Lord, not from Sara, but from Mary," Ambrose wrote, "...because she is a virgin not only uncorrupted, but a virgin untouched by any stain of sin...".

With regard to the Eucharist, (writing circa 390 A.D.), St. Ambrose explained in his *"De Sacrementis"* (literally - On the Sacraments) when, and how, Christ becomes present in the Eucharist. In the fourth book of his treatise, he wrote:

"...But that bread is bread before the words of the Sacrament; but when the consecration is added, what is bread becomes the flesh of Christ..." therefore, the words of Christ makes this a Sacrament.

The Sign of the Cross, along with all other uses of the cruciform image in the symbolism of the church, developed out of spontaneous devotional practices of early Christians. At first, the cross was traced in its entirety on the forehead alone, with the thumb of the right hand.

Gradually the forehead sign was applied to other parts of the body. There is evidence of this development in the writing of St. Ambrose.

On Matters of the State

In 388 AD., Theodosius became sole emperor of East and West. He delivered the deathblow to Paganism with his decrees in 391 A.D. and 392 A.D. forbidding Pagan worship and demanding Christian orthodoxy in union with the Pope.

He was not all-powerful, however, for St. Ambrose Bishop of Milan successfully defended the superiority of the church's power over that of the State.

Ambrose threatened him with excommunication unless he did penance publicly for the massacres of a large group of Thessalonians who had rebelled in 390 A.D. Theodosius finally yielded and did penance. This incident was an important milestone in church-state relationship. In addition to his many other accomplishments, one of St. Ambrose's greatest accomplishments was the conversion of St. Augustine.

ST. AUGUSTINE

The greatest of the early fathers of the western church was St. Augustine, born at Tagaste in North Africa on November 13, 354 AD. His father Patricius, a landholder and town councilor, was a Pagan through most of his life.

Augustine's mother, St. Monica, was instrumental in the conversion of both father and son to Christianity.

St. Ambrose Archbishop of Milan also played an influential part in Augustine's conversion. Bishop of Hippo - which is near Tagaste - from 395 A.D., Augustine died at Hippo on August 28, 430 A.D.

North Africa was then a part of the Roman Empire. To its citizens, the Roman empire meant the civilized world. It covered all the lands bordering on the Mediterranean Sea as well as a large portion of the Island of Britain to the North. Augustine grew up, lived, and labored in a Latin culture, close to the center of Western Civilization.

At age 17, he went to Carthage to study rhetoric. Succumbing to some extent to the immoral influences in that city, he led a life for which he later expressed regret and remorse in his "Confessions". After finishing his studies there, he taught rhetoric's at Tagasate and at Carthage. From the sensual life of his student days in Carthage, Augustine swung to the other extreme, Manichaeism.

The Manicheans were members of a religious sect, which considered all material things evil. Becoming disillusioned with Manichaeism, he soon was skeptical of all religious beliefs.

In 383 A.D., he went to Rome for a short while. After a few months, he went to Milan as a teacher of rhetoric.

Milan was then the seat of the emperor's court and the bishopric of St. Ambrose. The arguments of St. Ambrose helped him to arrive at belief in Christ. He was baptized in 387.

Abandoning a worldly political career, which was then opening up to him, Augustine returned to Africa, became a priest in 391 A.D. and bishop of Hippo in 395 A.D.

His great writings were done 42 years after his conversion. The known writings of St. Augustine comprise 113 books, 218 letters, and 500 sermons.

The letters generally show him to have been in communication with people of every station all over the Roman world. Both letters and sermons show his ready understanding of the problems of men and his confidence of their Christian solution.

His works may be classified as controversial or non-controversial, depending upon whether or not they involved debate with Heretics.

Controversial Works:

(Against the Manicheans)

"On the usefulness of believing; against Faustus the Manichee; against Secundinus. "

He established the credibility of the Bible. The existence of moral evil in man could be explained without supposing that there was an evil supreme being in addition to the good God.

(Against the Donatist)

"On Baptism against the Donatist" the church in Africa was split in two with nearly every See having two Bishops, a Catholic, and a

Donatist. Augustine explained and elaborated Catholic teaching on the nature of the Church and of its Sacraments.

The most tragic controversy of all, however, was that with the Pelagians.

Non-controversial:

The "Dialogues" reflect the general interests of an intellectual who has undergone the experience of conversion.

The "Confessions" is not without its difficulties. While it is true that the confession of sin is a prominent and fundamental element in it, the work is also meant to be a "confession" or proclamation of God's existence and glory as manifested in the creation of which Augustine is a part of, the "City of God". The work as a whole is a proclamation of a new Christian era.

Augustine considers, in turn, the natural virtues of the Romans, the philosophical achievement of the Greeks, and the revelation to the Hebrews on the origin, history, and final destiny of man. He argues that all of these are fulfilled in the new Christian era.

On God and Happiness:

Happiness is achieved in the enjoyment of God. Enjoying God and one another in God; the peace of all is the tranquility of order God, the object of man's perfect enjoyment is one and unchanging. He is also three persons. Augustine attempts to describe the Trinity in human terms by making analogies to memory, intelligence and will, or mind, knowledge and love.

On Grace:

God is the life and illumination of the human soul. From the mass of men condemned in Adam's free sin, God chooses a number at least sufficient to fill up the places of the fallen angels. Original sin however, man's tendency to evil, is great and he needs grace. Evil is not something positive. It is merely not giving to God the worship that is his due.

On the Church:

His teaching stresses the Church's supreme authority. The marks by which the true church is recognized, he says, are its unity, its universality, and its love - the bond of its unity.
An inscription reads: "...*Some fathers have told us of some things and others of other things, but Augustine told us all, propounding the mystic sense in Roman eloquence...*".

Continuing now with our examination of the portrayals of the Church on the walls:

Viewing from the Sanctuary on the upper left wall is pictured, left to right, Elijah or Elias; center, a stained glass window depicting Jesus and the children; right, Moses with the Ten Commandments in hand.

ELIJAH or ELIAS

Elijah was the most popular of the Hebrew Prophets. The period of his lifetime was one of social and religious change (I Kings 17-19: 21; 2 Kings 1, 2). Elijah led the struggle against the idolatrous worship of the Phoenician god Baal, whom Aha, King of Israel, had worshiped. During Elijah's struggle against the Baalites, he engaged in a contest of "miracles" with the Prophets of Baal and stated that there would be no rain or dew except at his command.

After three years of drought, Elijah assembled the people of Israel on Mount Carmel where he demonstrated the supremacy of God over Baal. Then Elijah had the prophets of Baal put to death, whereupon the rains came.

Elijah reprimanded King Ahab for the murder of Naboth, the vineyard owner described in I Kings 21. The prophet is most often portrayed as being taken into the heavens in a whirlwind or riding in a chariot of fire.

Elijah is thought of as an invisible participant in the home celebration of Passover and in the rites of circumcision.

Elijah's Chair

At the ritual of circumcision while the father is responsible for the ceremony, the Sandek, or godfather, holds the baby during the ceremony. An empty chair is sometimes placed beside him; it is called Elijah's chair, reflecting a traditional belief that Elijah is a witness to the ritual.

Elijah's Cup

A sacred tradition maintains that the prophet Elijah will appear some year during Passover. A special cup of wine called "the Elijah cup" is set out for him on every Seder table. Before the end of the meal, the door leading from the dining room is opened. Someone goes to see whether the great prophet has arrived.

MOSES

Moses was a Hebrew prophet, lawgiver and founder of Israel, or the Jewish people. The story (quite familiar to all) of his life is set fourth primarily in the Old Testament books of Exodus and Deuteronomy. According to these accounts, he was born in Goshen, a part of ancient Egypt at a time when the Hebrews lived there.

Besides being one of the most famous national leaders and lawgivers in history, Moses was reputably the author of the first five books of the Old Testament, known collectively as the Pentateuch. He also authored other parts of the Old Testament.

Scholars agree almost unanimously, however, that these books are the interwoven work of many authors.

Moses is also well known to Christians. He is mentioned frequently in the New Testament. At Christ's transfiguration, he represents the law (Matthew 17:3) and the role he plays in the Old Testament is pointed out in the Epistle of the Hebrews, so as to offer a comparison with that of Christ (Hebrew 3: 1-6). He is also mentioned in the gospel of John again to underscore the role of Christ as the fulfillment of the Scriptures (John 1: 17).

JESUS BLESSES THE CHILDREN

(Upper left wall of the Sanctuary, between left side panels)

At one point, children were brought to Jesus so that he could place his hands on them in prayer. The Disciples began to scold them, but Jesus said, "Let the children come to me. Do not hinder them. The Kingdom of God belongs to such as these." And he laid his hands on their heads before he left that place. (Matthew 19: 13,14,15)

On the right wall (facing the Sanctuary from the Nave) St. Peter (innermost panel); then a stained glass window depicting the Scared Heart with St. Margaret Mary Alacoque and a panel in which St. Paul is pictured sword in hand, a sign of martyrdom.

ST. PETER

St. Peter was the most prominent of the 12 disciples of Jesus Christ. A leader and missionary in the early church, he was the first Bishop of Rome. He was called by Jesus to be a disciple and he became prominent among the 12, often serving as their spokesperson.

Peter was viewed as the rock on which the church as founded. He is pictured holding a set of keys, representing the keys to the Kingdom of Heaven, in his hands (Matthew 16: 16-19).

Peter undoubtedly had great influence in the church at its beginning; being consistently named first in the lists of the 12. The earliest image of him, however, is that of a remarkable missionary, not that of an administrator.

He was seen to have been entrusted not with authority, as such, but with a special vocation to preach the gospel (Galatians 2:7).

In time, the image of the missionary was shifted to that of the pastor. When the Bishop of Rome came to be regarded as the Bishop of the most prominent church in Christendom, the picture of Peter as a caring pastor was combined with the tradition of his martyr's death in Rome. This served as the basis of a theory of apostolistic succession according to which each Roman Bishop was regarded as the successor to Peter, to whom Jesus had entrusted the keys to the Kingdom of God.

ST. MARGARET MARY ALACOQUE

(Upper right wall of Sanctuary - window between the two right side panels)

St. Margaret Mary was born in the diocese of Auturn, France, consecrated her heart while yet a child to the most Sacred Heart of Jesus.

Worship given to the Sacred Heart is a special form of devotion to Jesus Christ. Devotion to the Scared Heart, however, looks more to the heart as a symbol of the infinite love for man, which animated Christ, and in fact, it is the very person of the redeemer who is worshipped in this devotion to his wounded heart.

St. Margaret Mary Alacoque is popularly associated with development and spread of this special devotion. In the "Great Apparition", the vision that she received on the feast of Corpus Christi in 1675 A.D., Christ appeared to her and showed her his wounded heart and said," Behold this heart burning with so great a love for men."

The practice of First Friday devotion has its origin in the appearances of Christ to St. Margaret Mary in the 17th Century. St. Margaret Mary was asked by our Lord to receive Communion on the First Friday of each month in reparation for the resistance of men to his love. The usual practice is to hear Mass, received Communion or reparation and attend a Holy Hour.

The Holy Hour is a pious exercise composed of both mental and vocal prayer. There is no specific formula of prayers that must be recited and no definite time at which a Holy Hour must be observed.

ST. PAUL

St. Paul is called the greatest missionary of Christianity and its first Theologian. He was called to be the apostle to the Gentiles, but was born to Jewish parents in a thoroughly observant home in Tarsus. In all respects, he was reared in accordance with the Pharisaic interpretation of the law.

Paul's letters reflect a keen knowledge of Greek rhetoric, something he doubtless learned as a youth in Tarsus. However, his patterns of thought also reflect formal training in the Jewish law as preparation for becoming a Rabbi.

By his own account, Paul excelled in the study of the law (Galatians 1:14 Philistines 3-6) and his zeal for it led him to persecute the Christian church, holding it to be a Jewish sect that was untrue to the law and that should therefore be destroyed (Galatians 1:13). Acts portrays him as a supportive witness to the stoning of St. Stephen the first Christian martyr.

Paul became a Christian after experiencing a vision of Christ during a journey from Jerusalem to Damascus (Acts 9:1-19; 22:5-16; 26:12-18).

Paul viewed his call to be a Christian and his call to be an evangelist to the Gentiles as a single and indivisible event. He was convinced that Christianity was God's call to the entire world and that God was making this call apart from the requirement of the Jewish law.

Scarcely any part of Paul's thought has been more widely misunderstood than that which involved the terms flesh and spirit. These are not to be understood as simply the constituent parts of a human being; for Paul they were conflicting spheres of power because the realm of the flesh (the human realm) is susceptible to the power of sin.

The solution to evil, therefore, does not lie in a code of ethics that people can be exhorted to obey, but rather is God's gift of the Holy Spirit who triumphs in the life of the new community by leaving the fruit of love, joy and peace.

Everything is seen by Paul to depend not on the will or exertion of the individual but on the mercy of God (Romans 9:16).

SIDE ALTARS

Before we address the stained glass windows, which are on either side of the Nave, look left and right of the Sanctuary, to look at those areas, which were formally occupied by smaller altars.

THE SIDE ALTAR TO THE RIGHT:

The Celebration of the Eucharist is the focus of the normal Sunday assembly. As such, the major space of a church is designed for this action. Beyond, the celebration of the Eucharist, the church has had a most ancient tradition of reserving the Eucharistic bread. The purpose of this reservation is to bring Communion to the sick and to be the object of private devotion.

It is strongly recommended that the Blessed Sacrament be reserved in a special chapel well suited for private prayer apart from the Nave. However, if the Plan of the Church or legitimate local custom impeded this, then the Sacrament should be kept on an altar or elsewhere in the church in a place of honor suitably adorned.

The Blessed Sacrament is to be kept in one single tabernacle, fixed and secure. For this reason, there should normally be only one tabernacle in each church.

THE SIDE ALTAR TO THE LEFT:

Images displayed for veneration by the faithful. From the very earliest days of the church, there has been a tradition whereby images of our Lord, his Holy Mother, and of Saints are displayed in churches for the veneration of the faithful. The area to the left of the

Sanctuary is such an area where the statue of our Blessed Mother is displayed.

Technically, adoration or worship given to God alone is called Latria. When the object of veneration is a creature, whether angel or Saint, it is called Dulia. Since the Blessed Virgin Mary manifests the goodness of God more perfectly than any other created person does, she properly receives greater recognition and veneration than any other Saint. The special veneration paid to her is called Hyperdulia that is Dulia in an eminent degree.

Four prayers sung at the end of compline, the last "hour" or segment of the Divine office are salutes to Our Lady known as antiphons. These four antiphons are:

__Alma Redemptoris Mater__: used for the beginning of Advent to Candlemas

__Ave Regina Coelorum__: from Candlemas to Holy Thursday

__Regina Coeli__: during Eastertide

 __Salve Regina__: from Trinity Sunday to Advent.

A devotion held three times a day - morning, noon, and evening - that commemorates the mystery of the incarnation is known as the Angelus. It is generally classified as a devotion to the Blessed Virgin Mary. Some others that have a wide current popularity either in parts or all of the world include prayers such as the Rosary; Sacramentals or devotional objects such as Scapulas; places of Pilgrimage such as Fatima; and associations such as the Legion of Mary. Usually the private devotion is related to the liturgical one.

THE WINDOWS

As previously stated, liturgy's climate is one of awe, mystery, wonder, reverence, thanksgiving and praise. Therefore, it cannot be satisfied with anything less than the beautiful in its environment. The stained glass windows, which grace the church of St Francis of Assisi, are both instructional and beautiful in their own right.

ST. CLAIRE OF ASSISI – (First window on the right side)

A follower of St Francis of Assisi and a foundress of the "Poor Claires" (or Minoresses), she was the daughter of wealthy parents, born on July 16, 1194 A.D. At age 18, Claire heard St Francis of Assisi preach and began to receive spiritual direction from him. In 1212 A.D., she presented herself at his monastery.

In 1215 AD., St Francis of Assisi appointed her Abbess of the newly established convent of San Damiano on the outskirts of Assisi. As Abbess of San Damiano for almost 40 years, she lived a life of extreme fasting, mortification and poverty.

By her prayers to the Blessed Sacrament, in 1244 AD., she is said to have turned away Emperor Frederick II's Saracens, who were about to demolish San Damiano and the town of Assisi. She was canonized in 1255 AD., but two years after her death.

THE ASSUMPTION – (Second window on the right side)

On November 1, 1950, Pope Pius XII defined as a truth revealed by God that the Immaculate Mother of God, Mary ever Virgin, when the course of her life on Earth was finished, was taken up body and soul into heaven. Such is the dogma of the Assumption of the Blessed Virgin.

"…It was surely fitting, it was becoming, that she should be taken up into heaven and not lie in the grave 'till Christ's second coming, who had passed a life of Sanctity and miracles such as hers…Who can conceive that God should so repay the debt, which considered to owe to his Mother for the elements of his body, as to allow the flesh and blood from which it was taken to molder in the grave. Or who can conceive that virginal frame, which never sinned, was to undergo the death of a sinner? She died not as others die; for through the merits of her son, by whom she was what she was, by the grace of Christ, which in her had anticipated sin, which had filled her with light, which had purified her flesh from all defilement, she had been saved from disease and malady and all that weaken and decays the bodily frame…" (Cardinal Newman)

From her place in heaven, she still abides invisibly with us, ever our refuge, our comfort, and our hope.

THE DEATH OF ST. JOSEPH – (Third window on the right side)
St. Joseph was the husband of the Virgin Mary. Most of what is known about him is contained in the first two chapters of the books of Matthew and Luke. Several other passages mention him as the father of Jesus Christ, and a few refer to him as a carpenter or artisan (Matthew 13:55; Luke 3:23; John 1:45; 6:42). He was a descendent of the royal line of David and his family was from David's town of Bethlehem.

Joseph, Mary, and Jesus settled in Nazareth. There, Christ grew up in this household for twelve years. Joseph was apparently dead by the time of Christ's passion.

Both Orthodox and Roman Catholics venerate St. Joseph; the latter regards him as Patron of the Universal Church.

As pictured in the window, St. Joseph died in the arms of Jesus.

JOSEPH AND MARY – (Fourth window on the right side)
Joseph and Mary instruct the child Jesus at their home in Nazareth (Luke 2:40). "…When the pair had fulfilled all the prescriptions of the law of the Lord, they returned to Galilee and their own town of Nazareth. The child grew in size and strength, filled with wisdom, and the grace of God was upon him…"

THE VISITATION – (Fifth window on the right side)
Mary's visit to her cousin Elizabeth, which lasted about three months, is recorded in Luke 1:39-56, is known as The Visitation. Under this term, the episode is one of the Joyful Mysteries of the Rosary. The liturgical commemoration of this mystery is on July 2.

At the time of The Visitation, Mary was awaiting the birth of Jesus, and Elizabeth the birth of John the Baptist. The words with which Elizabeth greeted Mary, "Blessed art thou among women and blessed is the fruit of thy womb Jesus," form part of the prayer, the Hail Mary. St. Luke records Mary's response, "The Magnificat, a Canticle of Joy".

THE ANNUNCIATION – (Sixth window on the right side)

The Angel Gabriel's declaration to Mary that she was to become the mother of God is called The Annunciation. The story is found in what is known as the "Infancy Narrative" of St. Luke's Gospel (1:5 2:52).

Some believe that St. Luke learned the story from Mary herself, because her attitudes, thoughts, and words are so apparent throughout. It seems more likely that Mary shared her memories with the apostle John after Pentecost.

As the Annunciation scene was told and retold among John's disciples, his dominant thoughts were absorbed into the account, including the symbolism of the temple of Jerusalem as the abode of the Lord; the overshadowing presence of the Holy Spirit and the Glory of God.

ST. JOAN OF ARC PATRONESS OF FRANCE – (Seventh window on the right side)

St. Joan was born on January 6, 1412 A.D. to pious parents of the French peasant class in the obscure village of Domney, near the Province of Lorraine. At a very early age, she heard voices; those of St. Michael, St. Catherine and St. Margaret. At first, the messages were personal and general, then at last came the crowning order. In May 1428 AD., the voices told Joan to go the King of France and help him re-conquer his kingdom, for at that time the English king was after the throne of France, and the Duke of Burgundy, the chief rival of the French King, was siding with him and gobbling up ever more French territory.

After overcoming opposition from churchmen and courtiers, the 17-year old girl was given a small army with which she raised the Siege of Orleans on May 8, 1429 AD. She then enjoyed a series of spectacular military successes, during which the King was able to enter Rheims and be crowned with her at his side.

In May 1430 AD., as she was attempting to relieve Compiegne, she was captured by the Burgundians and sold to the English while Charles and the French did nothing to save her. After months of imprisonment she was tried at Rouen by a tribunal presided over by the infamous Peter Cauchon, Bishop of Beavais, who hoped that the English would help him to become Archbishop. Through her unfamiliarity with the technicality of theology, Joan was trapped into making a few damaging statements. When she refused to retract the assertion that it was the Saints of God who had commanded her to do what she had done, she was condemned to death as a Heretic, sorceress, and adulteress and burned at the stake on May 30, 1431 A.D. She was 19-years old.

Some thirty years later, she was exonerated of all guilt and she was ultimately canonized in 1920, making official what the people had known for centuries.

ST. FRANCIS IN ECSTASY: THE DEPOSITION, A VISION
(First window on the left side)
St. Francis envisions the Crucifixion. His love for the crucified
Savior increases. His prayers become continuous, he begs to share the
pain and suffering of Christ crucified and God now favored him with
extraordinary mystical graces.

THE RESURRECTION – (Second window on the left side)
In the biblical tradition, suffering and death were the result of Adam's
sin. In the Plan of God, redemption was to be a passage of man back
to God, a passage out of the realm of sin and death of this world into
that of freedom and life in heaven.
Man turned away from God by his sinfulness and was unable to make
this passage by his own power and so the eternal Son of God became
the Servant of the Lord. He assumed the same situation in which
sinful man found himself. He became like us in all things except sin.
He was the first one to make the passage back to God and it is through
the grace and power that he won by making this passage, that the
faithful are able to make it after Him.

THE GOOD SHEPHERD – (Third window on the left side)
When Jesus spoke of the true and false shepherd to the Pharisees and
said, "I am the good Shepherd." He was making a Messianic claim.
(John 10: 1-16)
There were clear prophecies that God would send a shepherd of his
own choice. (Ezekiel 34; Jeremiah 3:15).

42

MARY MAGDALENE WIPES THE FEET OF JESUS – (Fourth window on the left side)

Christ is depicted at the house of Simon the Pharisees. Mary Magdalene is wiping the feet of Jesus with her hair, after she has washed an anointed them with sacred oil.

JESUS IN THE TEMPLE – (Fifth window on left side)

The finding in the Temple, (Luke 2:41-51) "…On the third day, they came upon him in the temple sitting in the midst of the teachers…"

BAPTISM OF JESUS – (Sixth window on left side)

Jesus' baptism is recounted in each of the three Gospels (Matthew 3: 13-17; Mark 1: 9-11; Luke 3:21,22) and the fourth Gospel refers to it (John 1:32-34.) Its meaning is best determined by a study of Mark's account, the most primitive of the three, where Christ's baptism is presented as the consecration of Jesus as Messiah-King. It is the moment when he began his mission of gathering the people of the new Israel, thus inaugurating the long, awaited Kingdom of God.

ST. FRANCIS PREACHING TO THE BIRDS – (Seventh window on left side)

Of all the sermons that St Francis of Assisi preached, the one to the birds is certainly one of the most beautiful ever preached on Earth. "…Because everything comes from the same source…" wrote St. Bonaventure. Francis sensed the kinship, which exists between men, animals, plants, the sea, and the stars.

"...Did not Christ himself, speak of the goodness of the heavenly Father who gives the sparrow its food and the lily of the fields its brilliant garb? And before sin came into the world did not men, beasts, and the elements live in harmony?"

However, no one in the West ever experienced or expressed as did St. Frances such a feeling of the universal brotherhood of all creation.

<u>ST. FRANCIS OF ASSISI</u> Il Poverello (Little Poor Man)

Often described as the most beloved Saint in the calendar of the church, St. Francis exercised great influence on Christian and non-Christians alike. He founded, almost in spite of himself, the order of the Franciscans.

He is said to have saved the medieval Church from decay and infused new life into it. No one of his century surpassed him in service.

He was born Giovanni Bernadone in Assisi in 1182 A.D. and died on October 3, 1226 A.D. at his chapel about two miles from his birthplace.

His mother, Pica, had the newborn baby carried to the baptismal font of San Rufino church where he was christened John. "It was the father", the three companions said, "who in his joy, had him named Francis on his return from his far journey".

Peter Benardone, father of the future Saint, was one of the richest cloth merchants in the city, yet Francis' biographers have noted that he was a man without learning. He studied neither theology non

Canon law and was unversed in any of the Ecclesiastical or Profane Sciences of the time.

So how was it that France and the French people adopted this Italian born "Little Poor Man" as its Saint?

His father knew French and no doubt taught it to his son, for French at that time served as a business language everywhere in the West. His father, no doubt, had his sons growing up in the business and of course, French was a language they should know.

Thomas of Celano, the earliest of Francis' biographers, observes that "It was always in French that St. Francis expressed himself when he was filled with the Holy Spirit as if he had foreseen the special cult with which France was to honor him one day and wanted to show himself grateful in advance".

Francis often affirmed that he was born a commoner. In an attempt to have Francis born into nobility, French historians have his mother being born in Provence from the illustrious house of Bourlement - none of this has ever been verified. "In the name of our Lord Jesus Christ, of his glorious Mother, and of all the Saints," said Francis joyously, "I choose the Province of France. For the French are especially dear to me, because they have a greater reverence than that of other people for the Holy Eucharist."

The life and events of St. Francis would fill volumes (Bibliography). So much of his life can be considered the example to follow that writers and especially artists became competitive to express their individual ideas on what Francis' legacy to the world would be.

He renounces his father (for his wealth). He restores the San Damiano Chapel, restores San Pietro della Spina and the portiuncula. He works among the lepers in the region. He evangelizes around Cortona. He tries to evangelize the Saracens; influences the crusaders, travels to Syria, and it goes on and on.

The upper walls in the Nave of St. Francis of Assisi church depict scenes from the life of St. Francis and followers.

Some of these scenes depict <u>actual</u> encounters in the life of St. Francis. Other are <u>reported</u> as vision of legends. It is well known that artists present their work as their own concept of the subject, therefore unless the paintings are from a world-renowned artist or School of Art; it becomes difficult with a limited knowledge of art to correctly identify the panels. So much has been written on the subject of Francis' activities that even the authors give different variation of certain activities as they occurred. Please keep this in mind as we offer the reader the following.

<u>**Standing in the Nave: facing the Sanctuary and looking right**</u>

Panel #1: A companion of Francis pleads for the life of two men falsely accused of a crime and facing the death penalty.

Panel #2: St. Francis heals the lame.

Panel #3: The death of the Saint.

Panel #4: Receiving the Stigmata - the mark of Christ crucified.

Panel #5: The Deposition - a vision of Christ crucified

Panel #6: Trial by Fire - Francis agrees to pass through the fire while the Sultan's priests all refuse.

Panel #7: St. Francis appears to St. Anthony.

Panel #8: Preaching to the birds – a continuation from the scene in the window.

"…There were some trees there," relates the Fioretti, "…so filled with birds that never had the like been seen in these parts, and there was likewise a multitude in the neighboring field…"

Marveling at this spectacle and filled with the Holy Spirit, Francis said to his companions, "…Stay here by the road, and wait for me, while I preach to our sisters, the birds…".

"…My little sisters, the birds", he said to them, "many are the bonds which unite us to God. And your duty is to praise him everywhere and always because he had let you free to fly wherever you will and have given you a double and threefold covering and the beautiful colored plumage you wear. Praise Him likewise for the food he provides for you without working for it, for the songs He taught you, for your number that His blessing has multiplied, for your species, which He preserved in the Ark of olden times, and for the realm of the air, He has reserved for you. God sustains you without having to sow or reap. He gives you fountains and streams to drink from, mountains and hills in which to take refuge, and tall trees in which to build your nests. How the Creator must love you to grant you such favors! So my sister birds, do not be ungrateful, but continually praise Him who showers blessings upon you…".

At last, he made the sign of the cross over them and dismissed them. Then all the birds rose together and fled off in the form of the cross he had made over them.

Standing in the Nave: facing the Sanctuary and looking to the left.

Panel #1: A man of Assisi prophetically venerates the young Francis – seeing him as a future Saint.

Panel #2: Francis works among the lepers of the area.

Panel #3: He shows the Stigmata wounds to Pope Alexander IV.

Panel #4: St. Francis in a heavenly vision, embraces the child Jesus.

Panel #5: St. Francis resurrects a young woman so she may make a good confession.

Panel #6:   In a vision, he sees the heavenly thrones.

Panel #7: The companions of Francis gaze in admiration at the Saint while he preaches.

Panel #8: St. Francis initiates Claire into the order of the "Poor Claires".

The Last Judgment

The choir loft area is graced with the last of our large stained glass windows. At first glance, it could be a little confusing with so many figures in an overpowering scene of Jesus Christ as King of the Universe in position of judgment.

Among the last of the public instructions Christ gave the people was a discourse on the Last Judgment, an exhortation to his disciples to prepare for it. Jesus began by a description of the commotions that would beforehand take place in Heaven and on the Earth; telling how the sun and the moon and the stars would all change, and the Earth tremble, and how after this an angel would sound the last trumpet and call the dead to judgment. Then would come the Son of Man, surrounded by his angels and seated on a cloud, while all the nations of the Earth would be gathered before him.

When all mankind shall have been thus gathered before him, Jesus Christ shall send out his angels to separate the good from the bad, placing the former on his right hand and the latter on his left. Then shall Christ turn to the good and say to them: "…Come ye blessed of my Father, possess the Kingdom, prepared for you from the foundation of the world…"

But he shall turn to the wicked and with an angry countenance say, "…Depart from Me, ye accursed, into everlasting fire, which was prepared for the devil and his angels…". And these shall go into everlasting punishment, but the just into life everlasting. At His first coming, Jesus appeared in poverty and weakness, but at his second, He shall appear as a judge, surrounded by his majesty, and backed by his power. The cross, now so much despised, will then be the sign of his glory.

Where are the Evangelists?

The Evangelists referred to are the writers of the New Testament Gospels; Matthew, Mark, Luke and John.

In our church, behind the Sanctuary, is a hallway, which connects the Priest Sacristy (dressing room) to the room used by the altar servers. In this hallway, there are three stained glass windows. The center window pictures two hearts in crowns – one the Immaculate Heart of Mary and the other, the Scared Heart of Jesus. To either side there are windows, which portray St. Luke and St. Mark in one window; St. Matthew and St. John in the other window.

Tradition identifies these writers by the following symbols or emblems.

St. Matthew is represented by a young man because he emphasizes through his Gospel the human nature of our Lord.

St. Mark's emblem is the lion, king of the desert, beast, for he begins his Gospel with St. John the Baptist- the voice of one who cries in the wilderness.

St. Luke is shown as the ox; a sacrificial beast. His Gospel opens with the account of Zachary who is priest of the temple.

St. John is represented as an eagle who alone can gaze upon the sun. His Gospel begins with - and accents - the divine nature of Christ.

A Few Facts on the Evangelists

<u>St. Matthew</u> - author of the first Gospel:

His apostolic activity was restricted to the communities of Palestine. His Gospel was written to fill a sorely felt need for his fellow countrymen. It was designed to convince them that the Messiah had come in the person of Jesus in whom all the promises of the Messianic Kingdom, embracing all people, had been fulfilled in a spiritual, rather than a carnal way. "…My Kingdom is not of this world…" His Gospel then answers the question "…Are you He who is to come or shall we look for another…?"

He leaves Jerusalem in 42 A.D. about the time of persecution by Herod Agrippa I and tradition points to Ethiopia as his field of labor. Another tradition places the composition of his Gospel at between 42 A.D. and 50 A.D.

His gospel depicts the Holy city with its temple still existing therefore, it must have been written before the destruction by the Romans in 70 A.D.

St. Mark - author of the second Gospel:

He was the son of Mary, a householder of Jerusalem, at whose home the early Christians held meetings in the days of persecutions, (Acts 12: 12). St. Peter called him son, an appellation indicating the strong personal bond between them. He acted as Peter's interpreter because of the Apostle's little knowledge of Greek. He went with his cousin, Barnabas, and St. Paul, to Antioch from Jerusalem but left them in South Asia Minor (Acts 12:25; 13:5). Paul was unwilling to take him on another journey. but during Paul's first Roman captivity about 60 A.D., Mark was in Rome preparing to leave for Asia Minor. They became reconciled, so that five years later, Paul wrote to St. Timothy asking that he bring Mark to him (Timothy 4:11). According to tradition, Mark wrote his Gospel in Rome, basing it on Peter's teachings.

St. Luke - a companion of St. Paul author of the third Gospel:

Apparently, Paul's faithful friend during the apostle's imprisonment (Romans 16:21; 2 Timothy 4:11). According to tradition, he was also a physician and the author of the Acts of the Apostles.

The Gospel itself shows its author to be a person of literary powers. Little is known where they were written and the time is approximately 75 A.D.

In his Gospel, there is a steady movement of events from Nazareth to Jerusalem to Rome.

St. John - Apostle and Evangelist author of the fourth Gospel:

St. John was called in the first year of Christ's ministry because of his devotion to Jesus he is known as the "beloved disciple" and the only one of the twelve whom did not forsake the Savior in the hour of his Passion. He stood firm at the cross whence the Savior made him Guardian of his mother.

He is considered the author of the fourth Gospel, three Epistles, and the Book of Revelation.

Called the Apostle of Charity, he died at Ephesus at a very old age. Tradition relates that he was, by order of Emperor Domitian, cast into a cauldron of boiling oil, but came forth unhurt and was banished to the Island of Patmos for a year.

Our stain glass window portrays St. John and the imagery of a serpent coiled in the cup. This is generally referred to as the "Chalice of St. John the Evangelist" and is derived from the legend of the poisoned drink offered to St. John.

IN CONCLUSION:

"CANTICLE OF THE SUN"

St. Francis of Assisi

Most high omnipotent good Lord,

Thine are the praises, the glory, the honor, and all benediction.

To thee alone, Most High, do they belong,

And no man is worthy to mention thee.

Praised be thou, my Lord, with all thy creatures,

Especially the honored Brother Sun,

Who makes the day and illumines us through thee.

And he is beautiful and radiant with great splendor

Bears the signification of thee, Most High One.

Praised be thou, my Lord, for Sister Moon and the stars,

Thou hast formed them in heaven clear and precious and beautiful.

Praised be thou, my Lord, for Brother Wind,

And for the air and cloudy and clear and every weather,

By which thou givest sustenance to thy creatures.

Praised be thou, my Lord, for Sister Water,

Which is very useful and humble and precious and chaste.

Praised be thou, my Lord, for Brother Fire,

By whom thou lightest the night,

And he is beautiful and jocund and robust and strong.

Praised be thou, my Lord, for our sister Mother Earth.

Who sustains and governs us,

And Produces various fruits with colored flowers and herbage.

Praise and bless my Lord and give him thanks

And serve him with great humility.

BIBLIOGRAPHY FOLLOWS

BIBLIOGRAPHY

1. *The Catholic Encyclopedia for School and Home*; McGaw Hill Book Co., 1965

2. *Funk & Wagnall's New Encyclopedia*; 1981

3. *The World of Giotto*, c 1267 - 1337; Sarel Eimerl and Editors, Time-Life Books

4. *Saint Francis of Assisi a Biography*; Omer Englabert, Servant Books, Ann Arbor, Michigan

5. *The Golden Legend of Jacobus deVorgaine*; Amo Press; New York Times, 1969

6. *Bible History: The Most Important Events of the Old and New Testaments*; Benzieger Brothers, New York, Chicago, and Boston

7. *Assisi*; A Color Tourist Guide Book

8. *Vatican Council II - The Counciliar and Post Counciliar Documents*; Austin Flannery, O.P. The Liturgical Press, Collegeville, Minnesota

9. *Environment and Art in Catholic Worship*; The National Conference of Catholic Bishops, 1978

10. *Seventy-Five Years of Service to God and the Community: 1903 – 1978*; a commemorative booklet of St. Francis of Assisi Parish

THE END

www.ingramcontent.com/pod-product-compliance
Lightning Source LLC
Chambersburg PA
CBHW021919170526
45157CB00005B/2104